CW00829501

Mediterranean Gardens

By the same author, in English

Mediterranean Landscape Design: Vernacular Contemporary
Modern Design in Provence: the Gardens of Nicole de Vésian
A Garden Visitor's Companion
Pleasure Gardens in Provence: the Art of Michel Semini
New Gardens in Provence
Provence Harvest
Reinventing the Garden: Global Inspirations from the Loire
Bruno Lafourcade, Alexandre Lafourcade: Créations, Constructions, Restaurations
Serre de la Madone
The French Country Garden
Kitchen Gardens of France
The Art of French Vegetable Gardening
The New Provençal Cuisine
Gardens of the French Riviera
Provence: A Country Almanac
Gardens of Provence

Front cover: the Mas du Barraquet, designer Dominique Lafourcade
Back cover: The author visiting Antiparos with designer Thomas Doxiadis
Right: the Mas Dalmeran, a winery with Roman ruins
Previous page: La Malherbe, garden of Mireille Ferrari

Mediterranean Gardens

A Model for Good Living

Louisa Jones

Foreword by Dan Pearson

BLOOMINGS
BOOKS

The garden of Nicole de Vésian in 1996

The author's own multiple garden

FOREWORD

Three years ago, I was lucky enough to be part of a group of like-minded people that Louisa drew together to discuss the gardens of her region. It was a gentle tour of some of her favourite places that were united by the simple fact that they sat lightly in their landscape and made a profound connection to it.

A foreigner's eye always throws up the things that you take for granted at home and during her time living in Provence, Louisa has used her particular perspective to reveal a way of gardening that has grown through living in a place and responding to it with humility. The places we visited had evolved out of the process of managing the landscape within the means of the people who lived there and the landscape had evolved with the people who tended it without feeling overwhelmed by the hand of man.

Over time and in a conversation with the land, an aesthetic niche has been carved as a response. The gardens of Nicole de Vesian and Le Mas de Benoit are of particular note, striking this balance so very beautifully to borrow from their landscape, using what is to hand and working around the natural elements. Boulders dictate the passage of a path, and in turn the rosemary or myrtle is clipped tight to echo the surroundings. These gardens use nothing not readily available, with water applied only where it is required for plants to eat, the native vegetation integrated for the fact that it sits well and does do well there also.

This series of essays looks at the dialogue between a place and being part of it. It is a way forward that we should all be thinking about, one that draws upon the ethos of living within one's means and using the garden to connect wholeheartedly with the places that we live in.

Dan Pearson, June 2013
www.danpearsonstudio.com

Following page: Vésian's lavender tapestry – one clipped, one full

WHY I WROTE THIS BOOK

Beginner gardeners today have the whole world at their feet. Will they choose something Italianate or Japanese? Something naturalistic? Conceptual? Books and magazines seem to suggest that you can create any style you want, anywhere you want, if you are willing to pay enough for it.

Mediterranean gardening is much more than just another item on the list. It is a way of living in harmony with the earth without contrived effects or heavy spending. Born of long human experience on the land, it is frugal and fruitful, serves many purposes and gives many pleasures, year-round. Today it adapts easily to our growing ecological awareness, to individual creativity and community sharing. Above all, it perpetuates a long-standing partnership between human beings and their environment, tested in Mediterranean countries for millennia.

In recent years, historians and scientists have published a number of new books attempting to define what constitutes Mediterranean identity from pre-history to the present day. A new profile has emerged: Mediterranean landscapes have been shaped by human beings for up to ten thousand years. One result – a surprising and heartening discovery – is the extraordinarily high biodiversity that they still possess today. This cannot be wholly attributed to their geographical situation between the tropics and temperate zones. Scientists now dismiss the long-standing assumption that human beings have been degrading Mediterranean landscapes in a long, sorry decline from earliest times. Recent findings leave no doubt: in spite of undeniable disasters and excesses – many needing urgent attention right now – the Mediterranean experience offers viable models for a successful and sustainable equilibrium between humankind and the land.

Mediterranean gardens lie at the heart of this story. Not so much princely creations, though these too are subject to local conditions, but rather the type often called 'vernacular.' These humble 'home' gardens have always been refuges for biodiversity, places for personal collecting and experimentation as well as for neighbourly sharing. They have always adapted to changing needs and can be reinvented once again by us, for our own times.

Mediterranean gardening is as flexible as Mediterranean cuisine. Both have been deeply affected by the 'globalisation' of Mediterranean regions that began with the first Greek colonisation thousands of years ago. Yet each locality has managed to keep its own character. Cod – imported from New England for hundreds of years – is prepared quite differently in Lisbon, Athens and Boston. Mediterranean cooking grew from peasant roots but has become fashionable today all over the world, without any loss of local diversity. More than a mere trend, it has been widely adopted because of its underlying, enduring practices: it is seasonal, local, healthy and flavourful; it is economical but capable of great refinement. Mediterranean gardening has much the same base and similar benefits. It is time to discover it once again… even in the Mediterranean!

Louisa Jones, Avignon, 2011
www.louisajones.fr
Facebook Louisa Jones Gardens

I

WHAT IS MEDITERRANEAN GARDENING?

EDEN AND PARADISE WERE
MEDITERRANEAN...

In the early 1980s, I began visiting gardens in the lower Rhône valley, first to find models for myself, then to gather material for my first book, *Gardens in Provence*. I saw more than two hundred gardens of every size, type and description. And yet people kept telling me that there were no gardens in the South, apart from the *bastides* around Aix-en-Provence and the cosmopolitan Riviera heritage. Plantings were productive or otherwise useful, never purely ornamental, and therefore could not constitute a 'real' garden. The English model was just beginning to spread in France. Highly recommended everywhere were summer-flowering borders, lush pictures intended mainly to please the eye. Wartime rationing was still alive in many memories, so that the growing of flowers instead of vegetables was celebrated like the return of white bread. An ornamental garden, backed by a newly thriving business in chemical controls, was the only true delight.

And yet ... Eden was not an ornamental garden. Nor were the visions of Paradise imagined by ancient Greeks and Persians. In all of these, flavour counted as much as good looks. And the fruits of the Garden, as we all know, are very tempting...

In the Bible, we read: 'And the Lord God planted a garden eastward, in Eden; and there he put the man whom he had formed. And out of the ground made the Lord God to grow every tree that is pleasant to the sight, and good for food; the tree of life also in the midst of the garden, and the tree of the knowledge of good and evil' (Genesis 2). In Homer's *Odyssey*, King Alcinous possesses 'a large garden of about four acres with a wall all round it. It is full of beautiful trees – pears, pomegranates, and the most delicious apples. There are luscious figs also, and olives in full growth. The fruits never rot nor fail all the year round, neither winter nor summer...' The Roman poet Virgil imagined in his *Georgics* (Book IV) a model garden where every spring blossom ripened into fruit. The Persian paradise is also a promise of scent, taste, touch, love...

What made these visions perfect was the fact that gratification was available without work, eternally and in all seasons. But no true gardener would welcome this. As the Provençal gardener and writer Pierre Cuche puts it: 'No garden can be good and beautiful without a gardener who loves it so much that he or she finds pleasure in the very work that makes it all happen.' Fruit available in all seasons is something we know only too well today – in every supermarket. The flavour is not the same...

Another characteristic is shared by all these visions of paradise: they are all Mediterranean...

This is gardening, that gives
us useful ornament for our
household, countless species
of root, herb, flower and fruit,
with many marvels…

Olivier de Serres,
southern French agronomist, 1600.

A MOVING MOSAIC

A new generation of ecologically-minded historians and scientists concerned with history has been examining the factors defining Mediterranean identity since earliest times. All agree that these regions are characterised by an exceptional fragmentation. Taken together, they constitute a mosaic of small localities in constant evolution. Just as with language dialects or cooking, each place has its own, unique character but remains part of a coherent whole. The sub-divisions are first of all geological and topographical, the result of terrestrial upheavals that created the numerous islands and mountains of this inland sea. These in turn create many small microclimates within the overall norm – for this zone – of long, dry summers and mild, wet winters. The Mediterranean is also known, more than other regions, for the violence of its weather: wind storms, floods, fires, heat waves, cold snaps and droughts may be extreme in one place while scarcely touching neighbouring communities. The British historians Peregrine Horden and Nicholas Purcell define the Mediterranean 'in terms of the unpredictable, the variable and above all the local'. They cite the English poet W. H. Auden who, in his poem 'In Praise of Limestone', admired 'this region of short distances and definite places […] Adjusted to the local needs of valleys/ Where everything can be touched or reached by walking.'

Life has never been easy in such conditions, but this same fragmentation offers humankind a wide range of resources. Farming has never been more than one possibility among others and not always the main one. Humans constantly discover and invent new ways of dealing with the raw materials nature provides. Plants and animal substances turn into dyes, textiles, perfumes, drugs; clay becomes utensils, building materials, whole houses; metals become tools but also luxury items, the object of intensive trading from earliest times. The sea is never far away. Hesiod, the peasant bard of ancient Greece, recommended that his colleagues work the land in the winter and become sailors in summer. Horden and Purcell reject the conventional image of self-sufficient peasant communities and insist on 'connectivity' from earliest times. Survival in these regions, they claim, always depended on markets. The least gardener traded surpluses with neighbours, including those in nearby villages. Commerce and even industry are now thought to be older than previously imagined. Stone seals recently dug up in Syria at the settlement of Tell Zeidan, seven thousand years old, were apparently used to mark goods for sale elsewhere. There were also smelting workshops that used copper mined four hundred kilometres away. The wheel had not yet been invented, nor transport by donkey…

The same historians judge that 'The Mediterranean garden is a more typical image of primary production than the wheat field or the grazed hillside. Diversity of labour, technique or intensity, as well as of the quality and quantity of what is tended on the small scale, are structural features of Mediterranean history.' The French specialist Jean Cabanel notes how much vernacular landscapes owe to humble human activity: 'Man's omnipresence in Provence fills me with admiration. The smallest ploughed furrow, the curve of a country road, a bit of drystone walling, each of these reveals a gesture, a reflection in deep harmony with the spirit of place.'

O for a draught of vintage! that hath been
Cool'd a long age in the deep-delvèd earth,
Tasting of Flora and the country-green,
Dance, and Provençal song, and sunburnt
  mirth!
O for a beaker full of the warm South!

John Keats, 'Ode to a Nightingale', 1819.

BIODIVERSITIES

Mediterranean gardeners might pause to reflect that their soil bears traces of earlier human toil and may even have been worked for millennia. Northern Europe and other continents may cherish Romantic visions of virgin forests, tracts of wilderness undefiled by any human presence. But according to the authors of *The Mediterranean Basin – biological diversity in space and time,* 'apart from sheer, vertical cliffs and some remote mountainous areas, there is probably no square metre of the Mediterranean Basin which has not been directly and repeatedly manipulated and, one might say, 're-designed' by man'. In our times, when we are everywhere urged to 'tread lightly on the earth', what should we think of this long 'co-evolution'? Does human occupation inevitably mean destruction of the biosphere?

The same experts conclude that, current disasters notwithstanding, the Mediterranean rim is still one of the richest biodiversity hotspots in the world. They insist that this results not only from its great variety of soil types, land forms and microclimates but also from its human history. Diversity is greatest in places where land has been disturbed regularly but in moderation, in a variety of ways, and never for too long in the same place. Grazing, foraging, farming, burning and small rural industries like charcoal-making can prove valuable if they move around. Every excess of any one of these activities, carried on too long, leads to irreversible damage. This is true of flooding as much as of drought, fire, over-grazing or industrialised, single-crop agriculture.

As for the new generation of historians, Horden and Purcell also find that 'the human presence in the Mediterranean – humanity's co-evolution with the other species in the vicinity – is one of the principal elements promoting genetic diversity'. They refuse the 'ruined landscape' theory of earlier colleagues who, they feel, celebrate the rise of capitalism linked to an ideal of technical advance and dismiss Mediterranean cultures, both ancient and modern, as backward and decadent. Horden and Purcell defend a vision that is not linear and progressive but recurrent. While they admit that 'Mediterranean regions have seen many episodes of 'environmental degradation directly caused by human action, sometimes irreversibly', they insist that 'local and periodic episodes will usually resist incorporation into larger tendencies or processes, such as those identified with "economic growth" and, equally, occasional and sporadic phases of abatement should not be soldered together to construct a vision of "decline"'. History, they assert, always reveals flux: 'There is no "balanced arcadia", no ecological state of grace that can protect the capacity for life and resilience that characterise Mediterranean regions.' They recommend, however, some very positive models that we badly need to explore and implement today. Every gardener, by his or her choice of seeds, tools, fertilisers and techniques, participates in the protection of 'the capacity of life and resilience' for future generations.

We inhabit a small portion of the earth … living round the sea like ants and frogs round a pond.

Socrates, in Plato's *Phaedo*, 5th century B.C.

Exotic gardening at Cap Ferrat

II

USEFUL, GOOD
AND GOOD-LOOKING

VERNACULAR GARDENING

Garden historians sometimes assume that peasant gardens had no aesthetic appeal because their primary aim was to produce food. What is useful cannot be beautiful. And yet the kind of peasant architecture called 'vernacular', found all over Europe, is often admired precisely because its beauty is functional and skilfully adapted to local conditions. With all our sophistication, we rarely match today the simple elegance and harmony of those anonymous builders working in difficult conditions. Why refuse to acknowledge that the same people might also have enjoyed the beauty of their gardens? Why deny them pride of workmanship, a capacity for invention, for grass roots 'make-do'? The most humble garden expresses someone's dream. The painter Van Gogh made no mistake when, in 1889, he admired 'these farmhouse gardens with the lovely big red Provence roses, the vines, the fig trees; it's all so poetic!'.

In the Mediterranean, the line between family gardening and small-scale multi-crop farming is often hard to draw. In both cases, variety hedges against the failure of any single yield. And if rotation means constant change for any one plot or field, the whole balance stays much the same over time, fragile but tenacious. Daily adaptability to the 'unpredictable, the variable and above all the local' requires constant ingenuity. 'Do things yourself with whatever you have, that's the peasant tradition,' says Provençal gardener Doudou Bayol.

Sustainability is the result of a deep knowledge of local conditions and resourcefulness in putting them to good use.

The opposite extreme is exotic, cosmopolitan fashion, here today and gone tomorrow. The most famous early instance was the tulip mania in Holland in the seventeenth century, when this hitherto unknown bulb was first imported. Although some early buyers tried to serve them up in vinaigrette sauce, the tulip soon came to symbolise an idea of 'the poetry of nature, free from any vulgar utility'. No longer anchored by any real need, it quickly became an object of market speculation and ruined large numbers of people. An ideal of beauty linked to practical use can sometimes help us keep our feet on the ground.

Adrienne Cazeille, a peasant gardener of the Languedoc region, warns against idealising peasant life: 'There is no point preaching a return to a past that only those who know it from hearsay could idealise...' But she regrets that 'a civilisation that included humankind, where people were all at once a means, an initiator and organiser, has been replaced by another that excludes people except as consumers'. Today, however, in some places and at some times, rural Mediterranean communities are creating new social hybrids, mixing natives and newcomers. Peasant gardens become pleasure gardens and sometimes communal, more in keeping with Adrienne Cazeille's ideal. Although she deplores in her own region the kind of industrialisation that wastes precious natural resources, she leaves us with a fine image of a vernacular garden: '...frugal but nourishing, it is the work of a gardener for whom a few tools, a few packages of seeds and some plants suffice, along with a lot of patience and good will. This is a garden where nothing is discarded, everything is recycled. But it is also, very often, a garden for sharing, a garden of the heart.'

In the commonplace world, pansies were love tokens and fancies. From at least the Middle Ages, they enchanted people, stirred up romantic imaginings. In this they are one more piece of evidence against the conventional wisdom that country people were too busy or too stupid to have anything other than a doggedly practical interest in wild plants...

Richard Mabey, *Weeds*, 2010.

Left: Garden of Mireille Ferrai at Bormes-les-Mimosas
Following page: Garden of Doudou Bayol, Saint-Rémy-de-Provence

SHOW GARDENING

Every great ancient civilisation had its show gardens, opulent affirmations of power and prestige. Today, the Mediterranean attracts wealthy cosmopolitans eager for holiday homes in the sun. Luxury gardens offer much-needed hideaways for people under pressure, but also serve as showcase settings for extravagant festivities. These properties create a lot of work for local craftsmen but are often designed to a uniform pattern, whether they be in Greece, Morocco or the French Luberon. Their conception often defies the logic of place: nothing is more nonsensical than olive trees or lavender planted in lawn. It was long the custom for new owners to clear away completely whatever was already on site before planting. This situation is improving: those who take over working farmland now often continue production, maintaining existing vineyards, orchards and olive groves in order to captivate both the eye and the palate.

Some observers envy and others despise luxury gardens but they have one great advantage: they encourage enlightened patronage. Their owners often hire the best creative talents – architects, landscape architects, garden and interior designers – and let them experiment. At worst, the client buys a famous signature but never looks at or even sets foot in the garden. For such as these, many designers reserve their 'ready-to-wear' work. The opposite extreme is an owner so delighted with the results that he or she takes all the credit, never acknowledging the professional's contribution at all. But the best case is when client and designer really click together. This can produce real works of art, the kind that may advance the history of garden design. Another advantage: garden professionals often educate their urban clients in country ways and convert them, at least momentarily, to an appreciation of seasonal rhythms. When the British film star Dirk Bogarde bought a property near Grasse in the 1960s, he was looking, as he later admitted, for 'instant eternity' when he planted huge cypress trees. It took him twenty years, by his own account, to learn how things work on the land. A French film star, Jean-Claude Brialy, asked Mediterranean designer Michel Semini to make him a Provençal garden in one month for a big party. Semini met the challenge but, even better, he made a garden that lasted for years thereafter. The Riviera-based landscape architect Jean Mus observes: 'It is easy to make something sublime but the hard part is making something that will age well, and today the important thing is to grow old gracefully…'

One big difference between show gardens and more humble examples is the day-by-day experience they offer. The American novelist Edith Wharton, an astute observer, remarked that 'one of the chief advantages of being rich is that one need not be exposed to unforeseen contingencies'. Cosmopolitan garden owners often possess several properties in different parts of the world and move around to catch each season at its best. They never know the pleasures of the gardener who lives in the same place year-round, welcomes 'unforeseen contingencies' and discovers a new gift every morning.

What a country! The invader
endows it with villas and garages,
with motorcars and dance-
halls built to look like Mas.
The barbarians from the north
parcel out the land, speculate and
deforest, and that is certainly a
great pity. But during the course of
the centuries, how many ravishers
have not fallen in love with such
a captive? […] Submissive to your
wishes, Provence, they fasten
on your vine-leaf crown again,
replant the pine tree and the fig,
sow the variegated melon and
have no other desire, Beauty,
than to serve you and enjoy it.

Colette, *Break of Day*, 1928.

Garden designed by Jean Mus near Grasse

MULTIPLE GARDENING

The Roman gardener-agronomist Columella admired the *hortus numerosus*, which translates as the 'varied' or 'multiple' garden. He first observed that the humble cabbage 'o'er the world, to common folk alike and haughty King, its stalks in winter and in spring its sprouts in plenty yields'. He endorsed importing the best species from all over the empire, mixing local and exotic. He offered advice (much of it still valid) on growing plants that can cure many ills, help you sleep, awaken the appetite, serve to make or to dye various fabrics, give flavour to milk or curdle it, produce wine or beer, make whips, remove identifying marks from slaves, excite young girls or indolent husbands, and much more. Columella also recommended lawns but only in April, for 'the jousts of love'.

In Europe, if many grandmothers have perpetuated this lore (and perhaps these practices), much has been forgotten. Who today knows how to use the silica extracted from wheat stalks to sharpen knives, as they did in Syria seven thousand years ago? Inside knowledge means recognising that even species grown throughout the 'moving mosaic' vary their properties according to local growing conditions. One famous example is the lentisk (*Pistacia lentiscus*). Only the variety grown on the Greek island of Chios produces a resin known as 'gum arabic' or the 'tears of Chios', famous since antiquity for its exceptional therapeutic and culinary qualities. Gum arabic is used in the manufacture of soaps, varnishes, cosmetics, incense and the holy oils of the Greek Orthodox Church. It became an early form of chewing gum. It was considered so precious that in 1822, when the Ottomans occupied Chios and massacred the island's inhabitants, the sultan spared the gum arabic producers because his harem needed their product.

So many different plant uses can hardly be organised into watertight categories. The distinguished garden historian John Dixon Hunt, who usually studies gardens made for the powerful and princely, admits his confusion when faced with vernacular Venetian gardens, planted for centuries with vines, fruit trees and other useful species. He concludes that 'the term "productive gardens" is not entirely a happy label, above all because it posits a distinction between utility and pleasure or even beauty that is largely a modern one': modern and not very helpful, in that multiple gardening goes far beyond even food production. From its foundation, Venice maintained and developed its multiple gardens through commerce and exchange. In the Middle Ages the city became a leader in herbal and botanical expertise centred in its monasteries and convents. Later, Venetians founded the first botanical gardens in Europe to study the infinite uses of both local and exotic species. In France, unfortunately, local and global, official and grass roots gardening were already seen as being in opposition in 1258, when, by royal decree, humble herbalists were restricted to selling local plants while grocer-apothecaries could import and sell expensive exotics. This quarrel strangely resembles today's European conflict between grass roots seed producers and multinational companies with their near monopoly of officially approved varieties.

Oh, the triumph, the garden, a
paradise of the marvellous variety
of things and the sensations they
can offer; intimations of quality,
of moral philosophy, of different
arts of living and ways of being…
Oh, the heroism of the least thing.

Francis Ponge, French poet,
Comment une figue de paroles et pourquoi, 1955.

Ethnobotanical Medieval garden of Uzès, Gard

III

THE LOGIC OF PLACE

HOUSE, GARDEN AND LANDSCAPE

Mediterranean climates encourage open-air living during much of the year. Indoor and outdoor spaces intermingle: courtyards, balconies, roof terraces and gardens are extensions of the living areas inside. In vernacular architecture, if climate management was the first aim of every design, refined living also counted more than is often imagined. The French writer Jean Giono noted about fishermen's houses near Saint Tropez in the 1950s: 'There was no question here of architects, schools of architecture or even of Art as we understand it today. Never forget that these people were authentic hedonists! Their pursuit of happiness led them to understand that *sunshine is the enemy*! Their rooms are cool, their shadows soft. The rendered walls outside are coated with lime washes that reflect back the heat of the sun's rays away from the house...' The arbour gracing the southern façade of many Provençal dwellings offers another fine example of vernacular design linking indoors and out, practical weather protection and domestic pleasures. Usually it supports a grapevine intermingled with wisteria, both of which leaf out late in spring to let in the winter sun until the weather gets warmer. Both species then develop generous amounts of foliage to make a thick layer of insulation that keeps the house cooler in summer, while their two different greens refresh the eye. Wisteria has its long, sweet-scented spring blossoms that often repeat in summer. In the autumn it turns golden, while the vine is by then often red or rust-coloured. The grapes ripen visibly from day to day and soon add taste to fragrance. In winter, a well-pruned arbour is a delight to the eye, even when bare.

In Europe after World War II, housing developments sprang up in catch-all styles on lots that were bulldozed flat and coated with asphalt, whatever the existing topography. No consideration was given to the local logic of place. Today, new kinds of globalisation, more ecologically aware, let builders use newly-discovered techniques and materials to adapt to local conditions. There is often a real concern for the capacities unique to each site: slope, exposure, altitude, prevailing winds, the strength and amount of rainfall. Where a harmonious setting allows, a fine 'view' increases property values – a factor that counts a lot in the Mediterranean, where flat land is rare and many hillsides are terraced, opening on to wide panoramas. Architects, designers and gardeners treat such views in a variety of ways. The great Nicole de Vésian favoured the graded progression, where the eye moves from house to garden to landscape in a careful organisation of planes and volumes planned to mask ugly features and frame good ones. But earlier inhabitants, who lived less exclusively with their eyes than we do today, had already created a harmonious flow between house, garden and landscape.

The old Italian garden: free circulation
of sunlight and air about the house,
abundance of water; easy access to dense
shade; sheltered walks with different points
of view; variety of effect produced by the
skilful use of different levels; and, finally,
breadth and simplicity of composition...
Each quarter of the garden was placed
where convenience required, and was made
accessible from all the others by the most
direct and rational means; and from this
intelligent method of planning the most
varying effects of unexpectedness and
beauty were obtained.

Edith Wharton, *Italian Villa Gardens*, 1903

Left: At Roquebrune-Saint-Martin, Alpes Maritimes
Following page: Pergola in a Luberon garden by designer Dominique Lafourcade.

CLIMATE CONTROL

The Mediterranean is famous for its numerous microclimates evolving over short distances, thanks to variations in topography, exposure, altitude, soil types and proximity to the sea. A seventeenth-century observer, Mme de Sévigné, writing from Paris to her daughter in the south, exclaimed: 'How excessive you are in Provence! Everything is excessive, your heat, your calms, your north winds, your tempests out of season, your autumn thunderstorms. Nothing is mild or temperate: your rivers overflow, your fields are drowned and spoiled.' She forgot forest fires, volcanoes and earthquakes! The hot, dry summers typical of this climate zone can last from two to five months. How can a modest gardener hope to manage such extremes?

To shelter from the wind, farmers placed their houses just under the crest of a hill, never directly on top. The first plantings were windbreaks, like the tall hedges of cypress or cane still common today along the north side of fields in the lower Rhône valley. Every land form has different needs. Since the Bronze Age, hillside terracing has created flat surfaces for easier cultivation on steep slopes, creating spaces that are both protected and well-exposed. Mediterranean gardens usually need shade in summer, provided by 'roofs' of trellis-work, foliage or branches. Tall-growing deciduous trees planted in front of a house provide thick summer canopies but let in the winter light, like the trellis on humbler dwellings. As for water, its storage and distribution have been the object of intense study for millennia. Cisterns under the roofs of many country houses still collect rainwater. Drought strikes in one season, floods in another, sometimes without warning. Good drainage is essential: open ditches are preferable to buried piping to direct run-off at the base of stone walls. Similarly, permeable surfacing is best for lanes and paths, even stepping stones rather than cement lines. Seafront gardens must deal with salt, including the effects of spray on plants. As for fire… farmers rarely now practise the traditional land clearance by fire and grazing, so that, in the northern Mediterranean, forests are spreading. Clearance of undergrowth has become essential and many townships impose somewhat drastic measures. In the French department of the Gard, the same day in October marks the end of fire warnings and the beginning of flood alerts.

Sun, wind, water, fire, the sea – all these elements can serve life or destroy it. So may human action, badly judged, mismanaged or interrupted. Gardeners should know their local conditions and enquire about the strategies used in earlier times to deal with disasters or, better still to prevent them. For each danger there exists a range of resistant plants. Cypress and bay laurels are said to survive flooding relatively well. And it should be remembered that weather is not only a problem: living by weather, enjoying its modulations, is one of the great Mediterranean pleasures. Watching shooting stars in an August sky, for example…

… a very old earth, but harsh, has made the local farmer wary. He asks nothing more of it than it will readily give […] to protect himself against the inconstant weather which can still take him by surprise, southern Man has erected his fences, planted walls of cypress, of lance-like reeds, and spread out his tentative and uneasy enclosures…

Colette, *Prisons et paradis*, 1928.

FROM SEASON TO SEASON

The Mediterranean climate, its local variations notwithstanding, is defined by long, hot, dry summers and mild winters with heavy rains occurring at intervals from autumn to spring. Plants have several strategies for dealing with summer drought: some complete their life cycle before it arrives (as annuals or bulbs); others develop tough, evergreen foliage – leathery, hairy, spiky or thorny. By concentrating moisture as essential oils in leaves with a limited surface area, plants can tolerate long periods without water yet avoid rot in the rainy season. Many species flower in winter, then go dormant in summer. Spring is the time of richest floral display. According to the ancient Homeric hymns, April is the month when poor Persephone returned from Hades to earth: 'Spring put on its purple robe; already the fertile earth put on with joy all the multi-coloured flowers which give birth to earth's bounties.' Flowering orchards, carpets of wild bulbs and flowers, wisteria and iris – a Mediterranean spring is a play in several acts that lasts from February to June.

In earlier centuries, northern European visitors came south in the winter. The 'invention' of summer began in the 1920s with beach tourism, particularly with the American colony at Cap d'Antibes that included the F. Scott Fitzgeralds. In France in 1936, the beginning of paid vacations confirmed this trend, further advanced by the spraying of coastal marshlands against mosquitoes in the 1950s. Natives and enlightened newcomers still avoid the summer. Many owners of seaside homes enjoy them to the full at other seasons, then rent them out at exorbitant prices to summer people. To keep cool in summer, people now require swimming pools and lawns. Sometimes water consumption, when holiday houses are full of guests taking showers, mounts to over forty cubic metres a day…

How can holiday pursuits be reconciled with natural logic? First of all, by enjoying the Mediterranean in the so-called off season. For most of the year, the clear luminosity of southern air is a real delight; only in summer is it glaring and dangerous. Each month, each time of day has its pleasures. If a summer garden cannot be avoided, learn to appreciate the evergreys as much as the evergreens, foliage as much as flower. And why must grass be kept green? We love yellow as a colour in autumn, why not in summer? Olivier Filippi, author of a book on alternatives to lawn, advises: 'In the heat of August, there are several ways of gardening in the Mediterranean: lawn mower addicts will spend their days inhaling gasoline fumes to get a perfect green, compulsive gardeners will track down the shyest weed or carry endless watering cans every evening to keep the petunias alive. But the enlightened gardener will relax under an arbour between the siesta and the apéritif hour and do nothing else. He will have planted his garden with drought-tolerant species that need no summer care.' Among Filippis's recommendations are the genus *Phlomis*, especially *Phlomis chrysophylla*, spurges such as *Euphorbia rigida*, and the pastel blue of *Perovskia* (sometimes called Russian Sage) next to the acid greens and yellows of the shrub *Bupleurum fruticosum* – two plants that flower for a long time in July and August.

…the art of fitting in with the
seasons, the soil, the firmament,
the stars, the meteors, the weather,
passing time, and loving them all
in their fatality.

Marie Mauron,
a Provençal writer who describes herself as the
descendant of a long-standing peasant dynasty, 1979.

Poppies in the garden of Pierre Bergé, at Saint-Rémy-de-Provence, designer Michel Semini

MEADOWS AND LAWNS

April is the best time for Mediterranean meadows. The Roman agronomist Columella celebrated their many pleasures: 'Everywhere is fun and wine and care-free laughter; feasts are at their height in joyous meads. Cool spring's mild hour is here. So, too, the fairest turn in the year's whole course, when Phoebus' rays are gentle and invite us to lie on gentle grass. What joy to quaff fountains of water flowing through the rustling grass, no more chilled by cold nor yet warmed by sun.'

Gardeners and naturalists today take delight in the spontaneous carpets of bulbs and wildflowers found in many places. New residents have often been surprised by their sudden luxuriance. The British film star Dirk Bogarde, settling near Grasse on the French Riviera in 1968, later recalled: 'Almost overnight the whole area was clothed in tender green and starred about with a million wild anemones; hazed here and there with long drifts of grape hyacinths and violets...' Quite a different story from the uniform and heavily-watered green swaths associated with English lords on the same Riviera over a century before – or with today's golf greens! The first turf lover in the South of France was Lord Brougham who by chance in 1834 chose Cannes as the place for his villa, where he 'astonished the locals by his immense green lawns'. In 1861 the good people of Menton, wanting to give pleasure to English visitors, offered them pots of green grass brought down from the mountains. Brougham and the friends who soon flocked around him used to import turf in the autumn for winter enjoyment, then abandon it to summer dust. This at least was in accordance with seasonal logic, whereas, today, how many struggle to maintain lush lawns in summer? The claim is made that they are good for children, but as the Greek gardener Cali Doxiadis, former president of the Mediterranean Garden Society, points out, southern children have been playing successfully for millennia without lawns. She also stresses the inconveniences in the Mediterranean summer of the 'meadows' of ornamental grasses popular today in modern gardens. Once turned dry and sere, grasses represent a real fire hazard.

Lawns were the object of a recent study in the U.S., where the experts decided they were first established as a status symbol, proof of belonging to a prosperous middle class. Today in the U.S., according to the Environmental Protection Agency, private landscaping consumes a third of all the water used in family homes. The chemicals commonly used for their upkeep are so toxic that the Canadian city of Toronto has forbidden public lawns as too dangerous for... children. But another danger is that of rigid conformity. A seventy-year-old woman in Utah was hauled off in handcuffs for having neglected to water her lawn! The authors conclude: 'The essential trouble with the American lawn is its estrangement from place: it is not a response to the landscape so much as an idea imposed upon it – all green, all the time, everywhere.' This is exactly the opposite of the Mediterranean logic of place, with its respect for local conditions and character.

Fine water that readily rises as sap;
water that makes the chickpeas grow,
the celery, tomato, asparagus, eggplant
and pole bean, just as they grew in
Eden; water that can cook a leek in ten
minutes; water that you don't just drink,
that you taste like wine; water that wets
your stomach, rinses your kidneys and
enchants your bladder; water that lets
soap lather; water, my friend, without
which all these orchards, kitchen gardens
full of apricots, peaches, cherries, plums
would be nothing but a waste land of
stones and thorns...

Henri Bosco, Provençal novelist, *Le Trestoulas*, 1935

The Noria Gardens at Saint-Quentin-la-Poterie, designers Maurières-Ossart

IV

PLEASURE GARDENING

COLOUR AND TASTE

In the Mediterranean, hot sun concentrates flavour and scent in the essential oils that make so many plants aromatic. The same sun washes out colours in the garden, at least at midday in summer. Many British authors of the last century recommended only the brightest, warmest hues for southern gardens. They claimed that the soft, moist, bluish light of temperate climates allows subtle gradations impossible in the brash south. Pastels were sometimes equated with superior refinement. White gardens became fashionable; red, orange and yellow were condemned as vulgar. The presumed scientific basis of the original theory masked, in many cases, an implicit cultural bias: the Mediterranean was given to intense sensations and low tastes, such as garlic and those little rosé wines thought to give holiday-makers indigestion. In the 1920s, the great chef Auguste Escoffier (born near Nice) argued in vain with the high society of London and Paris to promote garlic. The novelist Colette, in the same years, felt it necessary to defend those 'glossy, highly-coloured vegetables, like the eggplant, tomato and sweet pepper'. For many northern Europeans, Mediterranean holiday destinations were places in which to enjoy primitive pleasures not tolerated at home, possibly illicit. The British writer W. Somerset Maugham called the French Riviera 'a sunny place for shady people'. Today people still like to 'let go' on holidays. And if garlic, tomatoes and peppers are now admired even in the north, conservative gardeners still associate bright, warm colours with vulgar excess.

In fact, many southerners also defend soft colours. They consider grey and silver as the keynote of southern European landscapes – the luminous grey of pale limestone, the soft tones of olive tree foliage. The Provençal writer Jean Giono insisted: 'Have no faith in northern painters who stick everywhere in their landscapes blood red, gold, and acid greens. Everything here is grey. It is the overall grey that brings out the soft whites and pinks of flowering almond orchards, grey that sets off the azure summer sky, grey from which the barely lemon tones of autumn foliage escape, grey that becomes grey again in winter... a strange grey made of intense light and colours all mixed together.' The painter Paul Cézanne, for all his earth colours, was fascinated by grey. At the end of the twentieth century, sophisticated gardeners in Provence were split into two camps: in the first camp, the lovers of soft pastels were often leaders in the fashion world, or at least those for whom form, volume, line and texture counted as much as colour. In the second were interior decorators and foodies, like the Englishman Sir Terence Conran, who made a point of vivid, festive holiday tones. But when the great English gardener Christopher Lloyd made exotic brilliance fashionable even in Britain, these distinctions lost much of their power.

What can be learned from this story? First, to mistrust trendiness. Second, to consider context. No red or yellow? Which red, which yellow, used how and where and in what combinations? We love these colours in autumn, why not also in summer? The colour debate centres largely on flowers – why not give foliage and fruit equal importance? What is the tone of nearby stone, brick or stucco? Above all, at what times of day, in what light will you see your garden? It is not the exclusion or promotion of any one colour but the balance between all these elements that establishes harmony.

What fine old walls gilded with
lichens shore up these terraces with
their patterns and lines of artichokes,
their stylish blankets of broad bean
beds or the blond mattress stuffing
of chickpeas and lentils. Yet from
the balcony where we look down on
them, these colours lose their interest
as food to take on the dignity of pure
pictorial values, and it is thanks to
the gardener's spade that we enter
the joyful world of art.

Jean Giono, 1961

Multiple pleasure gardening with Doudou Bayol at Saint-Rémy-de-Provence

GREEN ON GREEN

The traditional Mediterranean garden of villas and country estates is neither red nor grey but green. Their owners maintained for centuries a formal style composed of evergreen parterres and groves, using species that lend themselves to regular clipping. These included box, bay laurel, laurustinus, holly oak, myrtle, lentisk – each with foliage of a different shade. In spring, when new growth replaces old, the same plant may sport two different greens in dazzling contrast. Some of these plants have effulgent leaves, reflecting light; others, such as the cypress with its feathery foliage, absorb it. Many of these species make good hedging and many will grow in the shade. Green gardens generally feature a splash of floral colour changing from one month to the next – wisteria, iris, Judas trees and roses in spring. They provide a fine foil for the autumn colours of deciduous foliage – for example of plane trees, creepers and again wisteria. Earthenware, in the form of pots, tiles and paving, also provides subtle accents, but the most striking contrast is with pale limestone. The American writer Edith Wharton, presenting Italian villa gardens in 1903, warned her readers: 'Though it is an exaggeration to say that there are no flowers in Italian gardens, yet to enjoy and appreciate the Italian garden-craft one must always bear in mind that it is independent of floriculture. The Italian garden does not exist for its flowers; its flowers exist for it: they are a late and infrequent adjunct to its beauties, a parenthetical grace counting only as one more touch in the general effect of enchantment.'

Another type of Mediterranean plant, often low-growing, develops silver or grey foliage, though this too may change from season to season. Lavender is often green in spring but silver in the heat. Olive trees provide an archetypal example. The painter Auguste Renoir, who settled near Nice at the end of his life, wrote in 1891: 'This countryside that I always found beautiful dazzles me more than ever. Its aridity, with the olive trees that follow the weather, sad on grey days, sonorous in the sun and silvery in the wind...'

Mediterranean gardens teach the eye to distinguish subtle shades of green and of grey, but also of beige and brown, not only in foliage but in stone and wood. The great magician in this domain was Nicole de Vésian in her garden 'La Louve' at Bonnieux in Provence. A Greek gardener living in New England, Edith Wharton's own country, grew tired of hearing people tell her, 'I could never live in Greece, I like greenery too much!'. She finally protested, 'But which green? There are dozens of greens! And why only in summer? Mediterranean gardens are green year-round'.

What can be learned from a large, somewhat tatterdemalion Renaissance villa garden somewhere outside Rome? Look about and take in the picture: massive old trees, bulky overblown hedges, rough grass, tall columnar cypresses, crumbling stone balustrades, stairs, basins, statuary, urns, large empty terracotta pots, dripping fountains, pools, a mossy grotto, runnels, rivulets and brilliant sunshine. What impressions do these create? Overall the cool, dark shadows, varied greens and the bulky mass of the growth contrast vividly with the harsh light, and the garden as a place of refuge from the heat and from the workaday world emerges as the moving force at work on the senses here. The garden has a powerful, still strength that has the capacity to invigorate fatigued bodies and minds.

Trevor Nottle, *Gardens of the Sun*, 1996.

An old courtyard in Avignon

GARDENS TO BRUSH AGAINST,
ROLL IN, SNIFF AND SAVOUR...

S ince the early twentieth century, Northern Europe has proposed a gardening ideal of carefully arranged borders, blooming throughout the summer and unfolding like a series of pictures. Their appeal is mainly to the eye. To admire them best, you stroll past at a certain distance, often on a fine lawn, under an open sky. In Mediterranean gardens, the sky is not merely a backdrop for an artful composition, however refined. It is a primordial living presence – deep azure, studded with stars or unleashing a deluge. Its light actively participates in every garden, creating dramatic contrasts between sunlit and shady spots, sculpting shapes, emphasising volume and line. It constantly modulates space and can operate like a spotlight. Light moves through a Mediterranean garden, from hour to hour and month to month, as through a Cistercian church. Winter light is felt by many to be the most beautiful, almost liquid or tangible. In the summer, the sun's hard brilliance must be filtered, directed, softened or simply avoided at midday.

Mediterranean gardeners often play with vertical layering, using evergreen shrubs at ground level with deciduous foliage higher up to provide summer shade. Southern châteaux sometimes have classic parterres inspired by northern models, but their pattern is obscured by tall deciduous trees. The visual effect from upper-storey windows is lost, but you can now walk there in the shade. Mediterranean gardens often have such 'roofs'; they enclose you, envelope you, and may even surround you with scent. They eye still counts, but the other senses are also captivated. There are usually places for eating and drinking outdoors: some people are lucky enough to take breakfast on an east terrace, their evening apéritif to the west, summer dinners to the north and winter lunches to the south. Broad-leaved evergreen plants with rich essential oils perfume the air and add flavour to food, but they also invite you to touch and feel. Even summer shade is first of all a sensation on the skin.

Mediterranean gardens are very like the gardening model proposed today by the French ecologist Gilles Clément: 'I look too much for immersion and for ways of suppressing any separation between the human individual and nature to let colour, in spite of its immense power, impose on me the kind of distance required for garden pictures.' He proposes instead this alluring ideal: 'gardens not as a picture but as a density'.

Summer had returned, with its profusion of torrid days and fine nights teeming with stars, haunted by nightingales, refreshed by a light breeze which carries the scent of watered flowers...

Elisabeth Barbier,
Les Gens de Mogador, 1947.

Small courtyard garden in Villeneuve-lez-Avignon

V

GARDEN ART,
ART IN THE GARDEN

GREEN ARCHITECTURE

Mediterranean landscapes have been shaped by human beings for millennia. Ancient civilisations grew crops on hillside terracing, constructed complex irrigation systems, created trails for the seasonal migration of flocks. Mediterranean light also sculpts the land, creating theatrical contrasts between bright and shaded areas. The broad-leaved evergreens characteristic of this climate zone respond well to shaping into blocks and lines that exploit such effects. The seventeenth-century southern French agronomist Olivier de Serres recommended using cypress and bay trees for clipping because of their 'fine qualities of colour, scent and obedience that lead to magnificent works'. In historic properties, formal gardens regularly surrounded the house or château, taking their cue from its architecture. But these parks, unlike many of their northern counterparts, led the eye out towards the surrounding patchwork of vineyards, groves and fields. The productive landscape was not screened off but admired for its own seasonal geometries.

Foreigners in France often assume that all French gardeners dream of domination, whatever their region! But the 'superb pleasure of forcing nature' (as the Duke of Saint-Simon wrote about Versailles) is not typical in the south, where formal design is agricultural more than aristocratic, adapting by necessity to the lie of the land rather than imposing on it an abstract geometry. The human shaping of Mediterranean landscapes into regular patterns has traditionally helped promote growth, not arrest it. The example of hillside terracing is eloquent. In historic French or Italian show gardens, architects rebuilt the site to create symmetry with a hierarchy of spaces around a central perspective, whatever the original topography. In Italy, terracing made steep slopes accessible; in northern Europe, where such gardens were made on mainly flat land, slopes were created artificially. Agricultural terracing, on the contrary, must work with the given site, changing it as little as possible, and only to create spaces for cultivation. Its lines follow the existing contours, its paths are multiple and irregular, without hierarchy. Show gardens created an illusion of eternally fixed form; drystone walling, the usual support for agricultural terracing, is fragile, subject to the whims of every autumn storm.

Some garden designers today, like Dominique Lafourcade in Provence, use green architecture playfully, in open-ended configurations. She enjoys symmetry, but others like Nicole de Vésian work with asymmetrical, more dynamic design, rich with seasonal variation. Such art is not enforced on the site but suggested by its own character, made mobile not only by the plantings but also by the movement of water, wind and light – in brief, by natural energies. When the French ecologist Gilles Clément described the Nature Art of Henri Olivier in Menton, he praised the artist's ability to blend 'spatial exploration with the forces of life'.

My dream … to restore the old Soubeyran orchard as it used to be in my father's time … A thousand trees, and between the lines there will be rows of muscat grapes on wire; you'll walk between the walls of bunches, you'll see the sun through the grapes – and that, Galinette, will be a monument! It will be as beautiful as a church, and a true peasant won't enter it without making the sign of the cross!

Marcel Pagnol, *Jean de Florette*, 1963.

Left: Les Confines, by Dominique Lafourcade at Noves
Following page: La Louve, garden of Nicole de Vésian at Bonnieux (Vaucluse)

PRUNING AND SHAPING

In Mediterranean gardens, pruning may be agricultural, architectural, ornamental, playful or artistic – categories that often overlap. Topiary, however, is something different; it implies making the plant fit a preconceived shape that must be maintained indefinitely. Efficient agricultural pruning, on the contrary, works with the plant's natural growth habit with a view to future development. The plant is not constrained but thrives. Fruit trees and vines, if abandoned, slowly stop producing, make wood, dwindle and die. They need human care and live in symbiosis with their human caretakers, as do many cereal crops. This is often a labour of love: the plant sculpture Marc Nucera said of his mentor, Nicole de Vésian: 'She taught me that pruning and shaping could be very fluid, an invitation to touch and caress.' Marc prunes trees on site, foreseeing their future evolution over several years and taking into account their role in the harmony of the setting as a whole. He sees plant sculpture as always 'moving towards something'. Good pruning is as much admired in peasant communities as fine art in museums by urbanites. The Provençal writer Jean Giono says that pruning an olive tree well is as good as getting a medal. Pruning can creative for all sorts of people. Road menders often shape wild box and bay trees along remote country roads, just for their own amusement. Giono once noticed, on a dry hilltop deep in the back country, a whole park of wild box trimmed into arches around a labyrinth, 'with all the care of a sensitive soul showing off in solitude'.

Visitors to the Mediterranean are generally not aware that the plants shaped in formal gardens are the very same species that grow wild just beyond – box, bay laurel, rosemary, cypress, laurustinus, lentisks among them. For Mediterraneans, 'wild' and 'shaped' are not polar opposites but part of a continuum. Nicole de Vésian advised gardeners to plant side by side the same species (for instance lavender) growing free-form and clipped into globe shapes to give a tapestry effect. Many gardens in southern France have, in close proximity, laurustinus (*Viburnum tinus*) growing wild, used as hedging and sculpted for pleasure. The progression goes from natural to practical to artistic. The same progression holds true in the mineral realm: many gardens juxtapose rough rock, walls and buildings, balustrades and sculpture, using the same stone for all. Water can offer a similar continuum: springs and torrents, reservoirs or cisterns, pools and fountains. It is easy, near the Mediterranean, to think of human culture as part of Nature, not its opposite. Human intervention is a matter of degree. Our species uses the resources of the environment just as birds build nests.

...the familiar prospects of vines, olives, cypresses; one comes to believe that they are Platonic abstractions rooted in the imagination of man. Symbols of the Mediterranean, they are always here to welcome one...

Lawrence Durrell, *Spirit of Place*, 1969

MEDITERRANEAN JAPANESE?

Mediterranean and Japanese gardens are often compared today. At first glance they have much in common: both traditions posit a close connection between living spaces indoors and out; both prune broad-leaved evergreen plants into a wide range of shapes, and both give a great deal of importance to rock and stone in the garden. For both, flowers are secondary although admired; both value the presence of objects weathered by age and use; both 'call in the country' or, in the Japanese terminology, 'borrow' landscapes. Modern designers naturally explore these similarities: in France, Erik Borja from his beginnings and Nicole de Vésian at the very end of her life. For outsiders, this rapprochement sometimes bestows prestige on Provençal gardens that were long considered of mere regional or holiday interest.

However enticing the comparison, there are important differences. Japanese gardens are planned for a moist climate: their clipped greenery catches mists, raindrops and moonlight for effects that remain soft and mysterious. Mediterranean sunshine, present in all seasons, is sculptural and stark. In Japan, gardens feature rocks and stones shaped only by natural energies and not by the hand of man, sought elsewhere and transported. In the Mediterranean, stone is usually an inescapable part of the existing site, worked into walls and sculpted by master craftsmen. The 'borrowed' landscape in Japan is a series of carefully framed pictures strategically placed. Viewpoints are sequential, controlled, even ritualistic; sometimes you are not even allowed to retrace your steps (just as you would not play music backwards). In the Mediterranean, differences of level create numerous, multidirectional viewpoints – vertical, horizontal or diagonal, from a roof or across a valley. These are planned, used and enjoyed in many different ways first and foremost by people living in, not visiting, the garden. Above all, Japanese gardens are imbued with symbols. They do not imitate nature but distil it (Western gardens are considered very vulgar in this respect!). Their deeper meanings are designed for an elite – priests, knights, gentlemen (all male). Mediterranean gardens are earthy; they have peasant roots.

Nonetheless, the convergence can be fruitful and, as with many other cultural hybrids, can lead to a new synthesis. Both traditions play on a deep relationship to time – from the instant or seasonal to the age-old. Mediterranean designers today, like the Japanese, generally avoid centrality and the hierarchy of spaces imposed in the West since the Renaissance. They look rather for a balance between volume and void, near and far, often drawn towards a soft minimalism that can operate equally well in the tiniest garden as in large properties. Above all, there is a sense of partnership with nature that the West is now attempting to recover.

We live inside nature and are
a part of its cycles...Land and
plants occupy the human scale;
the sky is the greater part of the
composition. Another aspect of this
is the balance between fullness and
emptiness, shadows and light...

Fernando Caruncho, Spanish landscape architect

Les Clermonts, garden of Erik Borja in the Drome

HOME STYLE 'LAND ART'

L and Art (with capitals) was an American movement launched in the 1960s. Its works were massive installations in remote, barren places by artists such as Robert Smithson and Michael Heizer, who were fascinated by energy and entropy and disgusted by consumer society. Many of them felt sympathy with the Picturesque and Romantic movements evolving in northern Europe around 1800. In the 1970s, in Britain, a Nature or Earth Art movement sprung up around figures like Richard Long and Hamish Fulton, wanderers who left light traces on the sites they chose instead of bulldozing them. In both cases, the public at large knew the works usually through photographs. Today the term 'land art' (in lower case) is applied to any human shaping of landscape for artistic ends, for which the place itself provides the inspiration and often the substance. Writers commonly use terms like 'site-specific' or 'site-generated'. Gardens of course have always been both of these. They constitute an important part of contemporary 'landscape art,' especially in the Mediterranean where vernacular shaping of the landscape, often collective and anonymous, has been going on for millennia. The ancient roots of landscape art in southern Europe have attracted many international artists in recent years. Many favour mountain sites, which, though wild and grandiose, preserve vestiges of ancient human habitation. The public at large, once again, knows these works mainly through photographs, but they are accessible to hikers as Art Trails. Good walkers may spend a night in one of the Art Refuges made by Andy Goldsworthy in the Provençal Alps. (www.musee-gassendi.org) or discover the work of artists of many nationalities along the Sentier des Lauzes in central France (www.surlesentierdeslauzes.fr) or, in Catalonia, at the CDAN foundation (www.cdan.es).

Many of these artists explore natural energies as a form of dialogue between our species and the biosphere. They are neither imposing human order on raw nature nor losing themselves in romantic adoration. They are all fascinated by time, geological and meteorological, from the aeon to the instant. Like gardeners, they concentrate on weather, rock, soil, wood and water. More and more home gardeners are making their own land art with a simple pile of rocks or a dead tree trunk. Most today do not create an object as a central focus but play on the relationship between their creation and its setting, constructing a place or process rather than a thing. The creative experience may also count as much as the end result. In fact, any garden that is not a preconceived concept enforced on a site is already a kind of contemporary landscape art.

I try to understand the processes of growth and decay, of life in nature. Although it is often a practical and physical art, it is also an intensely spiritual affair that I have with nature: a relationship.

Andy Goldsworthy, British artist working in Provence

VI

NATURAL
HISTORIES

ROMANTIC, NATURALISTIC
AND MEDITERRANEAN

The first great 'back to Nature' movement was associated with European Romanticism, *ca*. 1800. Romantics fled urban and court societies to venerate Nature in the supposed solitude of mountains and forests, places in fact often inhabited. Famous landscape architects created an illusion of spontaneous Nature for affluent clients by constructing artificial landscapes, even moving whole villages. Mediterranean landscapes, associated with decadence by painters and poets, inspired ruins among rampant vegetation, crumbled stone walls, wind-bent trees, eroded rocks and grottoes, artificially created in northern landscapes that had not produced them. A similar Romantic logic attracts gardeners today to 'naturalistic' plantings that look spontaneous but are in fact contrived and often labour-intensive. Romanticism never took root very deeply in Mediterranean Europe, where 'unspoilt nature' is hard to idealise. How to imagine wilderness on land which humans have been marking for over thirty thousand years? Southern forests, scientists now say, were probably never impenetrable expanses even in prehistoric times but always sparse, lower-growing groves. In certain Romance languages (Italian and southern French, for example) the word 'woodland' counts more than 'forest'. Woods were neither frightening nor the refuge of pure souls, but intimately known by villagers who used them for feeding pigs, making charcoal, hunting, foraging... and as a refuge for heretics and outlaws. Today, on the northern shore of the Mediterranean, any site that looks 'wild' is probably abandoned farm or pasture land, 'old fields'. If it was recently cultivated, such a site may still be polluted by chemicals and its 'wild flowers' will be the kind called ruderal, that flourish only on recently disturbed land (poppies, for instance). This imbalance is not at all romantic and leads to landscape uniformity rather than diversity, one invasive species often dominating completely. On the other hand, biodiversity can be very rich on land that has known a great variety of human activities over a long period. These are the scrublands called *maquis* or *garrigue* and it is here that the most beneficial co-evolution between humans and other species has proved sustainable. This landscape can also be idealised, as a model for long-term land use. Romantic ecologists today often espouse an ideal of Nature as virgin wilderness, unspoilt by human presence. But 'unspoilt' in the Mediterranean does not mean land free of any human presence, but land that is not over-built, aggressively industrialised or degraded by over-intensive farming. Land that is still alive, able to participate in a dynamic process...

From weathered outcrop
To hill-top temple, from appearing waters to
Conspicuous fountains, from a wild to a
   formal vineyard,
Are ingenious but short steps

W. H. Auden. 'In Praise of Limestone', 1948

LANDSCAPE GARDENING

The Mediterranean mosaic is often very beautiful. Gardeners lucky enough to live in its midst often choose merely to maintain their land without seeking improvements, especially if they have a stable or slowly evolving ecosystem. Making a garden may just mean establishing boundaries with hedges or walls, though even there too, many prefer to let their plot blend seamlessly into its surroundings. The gardener's work may consist simply of keeping the landscape open, pulling out brambles and invasive tree seedlings. Keeping old fields just at the point where they are beginning to evolve towards forestland, the point of greatest species diversity, is the basis of ecologist Gilles Clément's ideal 'Moving Garden'. But preventing arable land from progressing towards either forest or desert has also been the main focus of human activity in the Mediterranean since prehistory.

Gardeners who like their landscape just the way it is can also be active in protecting wildlife, perhaps getting their land, even in cities, classified as a bird reserve. The French agronomist Claude Aubert, a pioneer in organic gardening, wrote already thirty years ago: 'Our garden is not only a place where we don't pollute. It is also a place where we try to live in harmony with thousands of other species...' To do this, it helps to know as well as possible the flora and fauna we live with, to learn about their lives and help them prosper. Gardens then become one type of ecosystem that nature lovers explore as part of the larger landscape. They can easily become reserves of biodiversity. The first botanical gardens in the world were Mediterranean, in Muslim countries as well as Christian, beginning in the sixteenth century. Southern European gardeners today are still more drawn to botany and natural history than to horticulture.

Any landscape garden in southern Europe is always part of a larger partnership that has been going on for a long time. Consider water management: the northern writer Gilles Clément once opposed 'natural' gardens 'where water flows' to the contrived version, those 'where water is made to flow'. The Romantic style does the latter, creating an illusion of spontaneous torrents and streams. In the former, the gardener intervenes, if at all, just to keep waterways open. But in the Mediterranean, where water management has been a great challenge since the earliest civilisations, it is hard to maintain Clement's distinction. The most spontaneous torrents and springs inevitably owe much to long-standing human activity. The naturalist-gardener aims at living harmoniously with other species, but accepts the right of our own to organise natural resources, including water, insofar as this ensures our survival. Technology is 'natural' to human beings. The point then is not to perpetuate a false distinction between 'natural' and 'artificial', nor to forbid human intervention altogether, but to protect all forms of life, ours among them, in a sustainable manner.

In this type of garden, we diversify to an extreme degree, we mix, associate, find just the right spot for a beloved weed that refuses to be exiled from this place of freedom, this living soil. This garden is all at once forest, meadow, marshland, hillside, kitchen garden, orchard, age and childhood. The gardener is all at once director and directed, never a master.

Pierre Lieutaghi,
Mediterranean ethnobotanist, 1980.

The Mas de Benoît, by Alain David Idoux, in the Alpilles

SUMMER-DRY GARDENING

All traditional Mediterranean gardens begin with a water hole, a spring or a stream. Today as water becomes more and more problematic, many gardeners are experimenting with drought-resistant gardening. Their model is the beautiful scrubland called *garrigue* and *maquis* in France, *phrygana* in Greece, *bath'a* in the Near East, and *chapparal* and *fynbos* on other continents, all of which share a common logic and exceptional biodiversity. These ecosystems are of particular interest to nature lovers and scientists because they bring together in one place all the usual plant categories – annuals, perennials, bulbs, shrubs, climbers and trees. *Garrigue* is not the same as abandoned farmland ('old fields') or brownfield or industrial wasteland, both of which may be contaminated by chemical residues. 'Old fields' can be anywhere, but *garrigue* is specific to parts of the world with a Mediterranean climate. *Garrigue* landscapes are usually subject to collective management by a farming community over a long period of time. Old fields are the result of one individual's decision to stop farming; if they are then gardened, it is again by an individual or family. Species that thrive spontaneously on old fields are often invasive exotics – pampas grass for example. *Garrigue* plants are local, usually native or even endemic (growing only there where they originated). They may even have evolved over centuries into subspecies on that very spot. They form a tangled web with similar neighbours, one that offers strong resistance to opportunistic invaders. For all these reasons, *garrigue* offers today an attractive model for sustainable, efficient, drought-tolerant gardens.

The person most closely associated with the genre is the Languedoc nurseryman Olivier Filippi who, with his wife Clara, treks all over the Mediterranean to study how summer-dry plants behave in their places of origin, often very remote. The Filippis try to recreate these conditions back in their nursery with a view to propagation and eventual use in parks and gardens in Greece, Morocco, Italy, France and Spain. They have evolved efficient methods that are much imitated, such as special pots favouring strong root development. The result is a range of choices that gardeners can adapt with confidence to very specific growing conditions. The Filippis consider that 'drought is a constraint that can turn turned into an asset' and they certainly prove this themselves with their own very beautiful experimental gardens. Besides saving water, their plantings need no chemical controls and thrive in dry, stony soil without fertilisers as long as they have adequate drainage. The Filippis recommend mineral mulches (stones or gravel) which keep down weeds but still allow for self-seeding. Upkeep is minimal; the *garrigue* gardener, says Olivier with some humour, 'replaces the sheep: he clips and prunes'. The result is a garden that is intimate, tactile, fragrant and with year-round interest. Home gardeners with suitable sites love it. As, more and more, do the people in charge of public plantings, and, in particular, traffic islands. Summer-dry gardening saves a community a lot of expense while presenting to visitors an image of Mediterranean character less cliché-ridden than the over-planted olive tree.

If your garden lies on bush-clad
hills and if, from their wooded
tops, no streams roll down, then
let a bed be raised on high-heaped
mound of clods together thrown,
so that the young plant may be
inured to grow in the dry dust
nor, when transplanted, thirst
and dread the heat.

Columella, Roman gardener agronomist,
De Re Rustica, 1st century A.D.

EXOTIC GARDENING

The Mediterranean has been a crossroads since prehistory. For the rulers of the first great civilisations, rare plant collections were a sign of prestige and power. Ramses III of Egypt showed off with pride his 'avenues shaded by tall fruit trees, a sacred way of ornamental flowers from all the known countries, soft and perfumed'. But even humble gardeners have participated in exchanges of exotic plants and collected foreign treasures: in 1889, the painter Vincent Van Gogh noted in a Provençal farm garden a 'figurehead depicting a woman in wood, taken from a Spanish vessel'. Ecologists today define the Mediterranean as a 'zone of interpenetration', known for its great density of new species as well as spontaneous hybrids, in contrast with more homogeneous regions to the north. Humans have introduced new species through both trade and wars, deliberately in experiments with the acclimatisation, domestication and improvement of many varieties but also, of course, inadvertently. In Lebanon in 1939, merchants traded amphoras made in Sidon for sheep manure from the mountains to sell to horticulturalists and tree nurseries on the coast. How many seeds were also conveyed with these shipments?

Early botanical gardens naturally mingled local and imported plants since their main aim was medical research. In the nineteenth century, the invention of steamships allowed rich collectors greatly to increase their experiments acclimatising plants from Asia and

America in gardens in southern Europe. Many species commonly sold today in garden centres owe their presence to these pioneers. Today the Mediterranean region still has some hundred great botanical gardens, forty-two of them in Italy. In France, home-style 'botanical' gardens with an educational vocation, mixing local Mediterranean and exotic species, have become a feature of agro-tourism. They are much appreciated by a public curious about their environment and plants in general, more and more aware of how much has been lost: in nineteenth-century Mallorca, markets sold 382 listed cultivars of almond alone. Today, draconian European restrictions – imposed, it is often claimed, to please multinational producers more than to protect the public – make it very difficult to preserve heirloom varieties. A new controversy about plant 'invasions' concerns Mediterranean regions. Terms like 'native' and 'endemic' apply to species, but terms like 'exotic' and 'invasive' apply rather to plant behaviour in particular contexts. These definitions are particularly urgent and complex in the Mediterranean where the heritage is already so mixed, the mosaic so often in fact a melting pot, changing so fast over so many centuries.

The notion of 'native plant' is quite subjective and depends on the scale, both in space and in time, that is applied. Everyone believes for example that sweet chestnuts are native to the Cévennes part of France, but in fact this species was introduced by the Romans to make stakes for their vineyards. It only developed as a source of food in the Middle Ages. But the sweet chestnut also grew in parts of this region several million years ago, before the last Ice Age. So is it native or exotic? Your answer depends on the time scale you choose.

Olivier Filippi, Mediterranean nurseryman

VII

LIVING WELL IS
THE BEST REVENGE

SLOW, EASY-GOING AND HAPPY

Is work for a gardener drudgery or delight? The French philosopher Anne Cauquelin, who has a plot near Grasse, writes that 'Gardening is a good example of everyday double-think; it makes us experience with constantly renewed wonder what in fact is the result of back-breaking repetition, as leisure what is hard work, as artless enjoyment what is the result of long planning.' Gardening also imposes its own rhythms: 'this slowing down that starts at the door of the house and turns our progress into a step measured by the pace of plants,' notes the garden writer Alain Hervé. It might be argued that the very opposition between 'work' and 'leisure' really belongs to the world of business and commerce. In the garden we work for ourselves. In Provençal folklore, there is a character known as the *fainéant* or lazybones. When Lady Fortescue began a Riviera garden in the 1930s, she admired her neighbour, Pierre, who lived off the honey from his hives. Her own gardener was Hilaire, so industrious that he pruned her roses down to the ground. Hilaire despised Pierre's 'laziness' but the Englishwoman noted: 'Pierre was perfectly happy among his meadows and fruit trees, with a few vegetables, his bees and his songbirds for company...' The Provençal writer Jean Giono admired further examples in the 1950s, 'widowers over fifty or young men just out of the army... living from a small olive grove, doing odd jobs ...' They chose to live this way 'to be completely free, to live, even to live well, at their ease'.

The pace has since intensified but in which direction are we charging? The Slow Food movement, born in Italy, chose food as its main focus but productive gardening is an essential part of its philosophy. Today it has over 100,000 members in 150 countries (www.slowfood.com). Slow Food fights the homogenisation of culture, helps people learn to appreciate their senses and, above all, to take things more easily. It has its critics: Silvia Pérez-Vitoria, a writer who defends traditional peasant culture as an inspiration for the future, admits that Slow Food 'helps preserve local heirloom varieties and crafts that might otherwise disappear and finds new markets for them'. But she feels that it appeals to luxury tastes rather than sobriety. In the Mediterranean, however, extravagance and frugality have always been closely linked. Cottage industries have always created goods for luxury markets – earthenware, fabrics (such as silk) or metalwork (including jewellery). Quality workmanship rather than expensive raw materials usually made the difference between the basics and opulence. Country people have long lived frugally from other peoples' lavishness, and still do.

The Franco-Algerian agronomist Pierre Rabhi, incontestably industrious, recently invented the term 'happy sobriety'. His ideal garden is based on recyling and he promotes an agronomy also based on compost that can restore depleted farmland on both sides of the Mediterranean. He writes: 'I never could get used to drawing a salary. My children are the same. It is a whole mind-set … I make my own resources and take my own risks.' The greatest luxury, and indeed the greatest freedom, is to have few wants and the capacity to satisfy them oneself.

This peasant, considered poor, has kept his good sense and his keen appetite for living... Accustomed to silence and a slow pace, his passions are simple. He has few unsatisfied desires. How many billionaires could say as much?

Jean Giono, *Arcadie... Arcadie...*, 1953

Le Jardin des Sambucs, in a small Cévennes valley

SIZE AND SCALE

The Mediterranean is a biodiversity 'hotspot' thanks to its fragmented ecosystems and also, in part, to its long-standing human presence. Its different soils, expositions and microclimates have proved a constant resource for local populations – human and otherwise – that also allowed quicker recovery after natural and social disasters. The Provençal writer Jean Giono survived the trench warfare of World War I before returning home. He insisted passionately that 'all of Man's happiness is in the small valleys'. Another veteran of the same horrors was the English novelist Ford Madox Ford who, in 1935, published *Provence,* a song of praise to his ideal 'Eden-Garlick-Garden'. Ford admired the peasants of Provence for whom, he felt, 'Nature is a matter of little squares in the orange, sun-baked earth'. This is 'land that has been loved – of which every clod has been turned sedulously and every branch carefully pruned until you have come to love your bit of land as you love a child whose every mental change you have followed'. These clods 'are as familiar to you as your children and the names of your saints, bullfighters and poets'. These two survivors both sought refuge in the small-scaled Mediterranean mosaic.

Today, many people still feel the appeal of the 'little valleys', especially with the current promotion of local food sources as a way of reducing energy and transport costs. More and more often, market gardeners make their produce available as weekly baskets or boxes to city dwellers nearby. At the same time, each gardener may experience his or her plot, whatever its size, as part of the 'planetary' garden imagined by ecologist Gilles Clément, who sees the whole planet as experienced as a vast garden, with all of us as gardeners. The agronomist Pierre Rabhi offers an excellent example of globalisation in harmony with little valleys: he grew up in an Algerian oasis, then emigrated to Paris but soon deserted factory life to become a subsistence farmer in southern France. After many ups and downs and several books, he launched in 1980 an international movement for ecological agronomy (www.colibris-lemouvement.org). He remembers: 'I started from a microcosm, my own small plot. Bit by bit, my ecological adventure took shape, like a growing tree. Bit by bit, I understood that everything is part of everything else, and that every tree is universal. I am myself a link, not a foreign appendage. Everything is interconnected, interactive, interdependent. There is no hierarchy.'

A garden is a small piece of
earth that requires a gardener's
care. It is also a universe for the
birds, insects, all the animals
that have chosen to live in this
particular biotope, in freedom,
in an interaction the reasons
for which sometimes remain
mysterious but which we know
are essential. A garden is also the
distant landscape that lets us look
towards the horizon, beyond the
hedge, beyond administrative
boundaries, and the limits of what
we can actually see, to the whole
Earth: the planet, our unique and
shared territory.

Gilles Clément, *Pour une écologie humaniste*, 2007.

A mountain village in southern Morocco

ECOLOGIES, ECONOMIES

Scientists who study Mediterranean biodiversity sometimes judge that this region is a microcosm of world problems – socio-economic, demographic, political and environmental. The Mediterranean also produces roughly half of the world's fruit and vegetables, but the old models of sustainable agriculture are disappearing: 'Notably, human populations in the southern and eastern parts of the Basin are becoming younger and poorer, compared with richer and older people in the north. Where is sustainable regional development to come from when you have huge natural resources and over-industrialisation on one side, and sparse resources and over-population on the other?' And yet, examining the history of these regions, these experts find cause for measured optimism in ancient models of agroforestry or agro-silvo-pastoralism: 'Here the three main rural activities of wood-gathering, livestock husbandry, and agriculture are practised altogether in a single space. Under this scheme, livestock grazes acorns or chestnuts and grass under open forest or woodland cover, while annual or perennial crops are sown between planted or protected fruit or forage trees, where they take advantage of the shade provided in summer. Many other possibilities for mutual benefits among soil, crops, and animals are also generated by agro-silvo-pastoral systems that, in effect, mimic natural ecosystems such as Mediterranean woodlands.' The actual species differ: the trees may be olives, argans, chestnut or fruit trees; the livestock pigs, goats, cattle or sheep; the annuals cereal crops, vegetables or even flowers for the perfume industry. Such a balance has, in some cases, lasted for centuries. The historians Horden and Purcell, quite independently, reach a similar conclusion: 'Mediterranean habitat mosaics are increasingly recognised as well-adapted and economically viable multiple-use agro-ecosystems for promoting sustainable modern development.' But they point out that patterns of 'colonisation' repeat themselves over and over in Mediterranean history, when a strong outside power imposes a single cash crop on a local population that can survive only by continuing to diversify (sugar cane in Cyprus in the eighth century, for example). Colonisation also imposes technologies that make farmers dependent on outside sources. Hence the proverbial peasant resistance to 'progress'.

Does this necessarily mean a conflict between local and global solutions? On the contrary, the *hortus numerosus* praised by Columella – the garden of abundant and varied outputs – can make international exchange the very vehicle of diversity, not an agent of uniformity. The historians point out that barter or trade of crop surpluses has long been a peasant strategy, especially where the sea is nearby. Many studies prove today that rural populations have long been more mobile than is generally supposed. In the Mediterranean today, those who move from south to north are immigrants, while those who go from north to south are tourists. The biodiversity experts, well aware of these inequalities, seek solutions for establishing a durable harmony between human economy and the biosphere, between small valleys and planetary perspectives. Landscapes given over to agro-silvo-pastoralism do truly look like big, well-loved gardens…

You cannot love gold and paper
the same way you love a tree.

Pierre Sogno, Provençal novelist,
La Serre aux truffes, 1997.

SHARING

In spite of their long history of 'globalisation' from earliest times, and in spite of ever-increasing abuses, Mediterranean countries have maintained a high level of cultural and biological diversity. When does a foreign influence impose itself at the expense of the existing or native configuration, and when is there a kind of fusion, a hybridisation that enriches rather than reduces variety, as with Creole culture? The Roman Empire provides examples of both, as well as of variations in between. Cooking and food offer a good testing ground. How differently has France integrated both North African couscous and the American hamburger? In their history of cooking and cooks, Jean-Pierre Poulain and Edmond Neirinck judge that 'the vitality of a local cuisine can be measured by its capacity to integrate new products in treating them in its own style, in its own "sauce" you might say'. In the international gardening world today, many associations and organisations organise exchanges of knowledge, techniques and ideas, much as monastic orders used to do centuries ago. Among the most interesting is the Mediterranean Garden Society (www.mediterraneangardensociety.org), founded in Greece in 1994.

Tourism is both the great bogeyman and the great hope. For the writer Silvia Pérez-Vitoria, a defender of peasant traditions, tourism is a kind of colonisation, 'an intrusion from the outside which rarely consults local populations and makes them adapt to the habits and expectations of visitors. As with the fair trade movement, in spite of good intentions, the effects are destructive where the initiative has not sprung from the people directly concerned.' Such tourism is just yet another attempt to 'undermine peasant autonomy'. One could object that, in the Mediterranean at least, trade and cottage industries have always helped preserve this very autonomy by contributing to the diversification of resources. If agro-tourism can help farmers keep working their land and encourage young people to live again in rural areas, this is not a defeat but the continuation of an ancient heritage.

Agro-tourism more and more includes garden visiting, a growing trend in rural Mediterranean regions. The old-fashioned vernacular garden was always a place for sharing – seeds, cuttings, harvests, advice. Today, more and more young people choose to make a garden the central focus of their lives. Often these are couples in 'hybrid' marriages – one local, one an incomer (might one say one 'native', one 'exotic'?). Opening their garden becomes an extension of traditional rural hospitality. They participate in local plant fairs and form or join associations which in turn become networks, supported by local authorities but self-determined. Many newly-made gardens are designed for the express purpose of receiving the public, to give pleasure but also to help people learn about nature and seasonal growth. Some are linked to a skill or craft (woodworking, drystone building, pottery-making, cooking) or a family nursery, or a café or bed-and-breakfast. This kind of tourism springs very much from the imagination and efforts of the owners themselves. It offers a healthy alternative to the industrial uniformity imposed by mass travel. It will most likely be a growing resource for those who inhabit, visit, or take inspiration from the Mediterranean.

This little garden is a charming place where use and beauty are inseparable. A garden full of attractions, which offers joy, shelter, food and relief from anxiety. A reinvigorating garden which captivates the eye. The work it requires is paid back a hundredfold! The person who cultivates it knows a thousand kinds of happiness!

'The Little Garden', from the *Catalects*,
1st century B.C., attributed to Virgil.

THE GARDENER'S NIGHTMARE

Agastaches scented with anis and peppermint
Lemon basil to rub and caress,
All gone...
Tiny, succulent wild strawberries powdered with dew,
'Pineapple' tomatoes gorged with sun and heat
Appetising promises...all disappeared...
Sunflowers turning their heads to the sun,
Cleomes so white and light in the air,
Cosmos, sulphur-toned, keeping company with velvety orange tithonias,
Stipas so cuddly...where are you?
The Gardener is living a nightmare.
Has she lost the way to her garden?
In the kitchen garden, no noisy clocks mark passing time.
She seeks out her favourite bench,
Her man joins her there,
They sip coffee, just a pretext for a little wooing, and...
No more bench!
No more room in this garden for her dreams and feelings.
The elderflowers break loose and shout a warning:
Peace and well-being are leaving, run, run fast, catch up!
I wake up with a start.
Nothing like a siesta in the sun to make your head spin!
The bench is there.
A fine coffee fragrance floats in the air.
The lotus flowers are playing in the water.
I know that tomorrow the garden will open its doors.
It is ready.
Tomorrow our visitors will come to share with us
Our garden of pleasures and flavours.
Of love and growth.
On sème au jardin.

Agnès Brückin, *www.jardinsambucs.com*

Agnès Brückin, gardener-poet at the Jardin des Sambucs

TEN SUGGESTIONS FOR ADAPTING MEDITERRANEAN
GARDENING TO OTHER CLIMATES AND TODAY'S NEEDS

1. Observe the logic of place and take it into account when you garden: for example, which way does the land slope, what are your local weather patterns, prevailing winds and rainfall? What happens to rain run-off? Do you need protection from flooding, forest fires, earthquakes or landslides? These seemingly obvious but often neglected precautions can save you expense but, even more, they can ensure long-lasting harmony in your garden.

2. When you are digging or planting, imagine what people before you have done with this land. Are there any interesting remains – old trees, stones, a hedge, a well? Or do you need to clear and clean, or even deal with earlier pollution of the site? Think of the past as well as of the future of your plot, however small. What can you add to its history?

3. Get to know your existing flora and fauna, even in a town garden, from season to season. Do they vary according to exposition, altitude, competition from other species? Are some plants indicators of particular types of soil? This can help you know what to add and save expense. What species benefit from your presence? When their aims run counter to your own, can you prevent damage without eradication? Avoid stereotyping: many songbirds are actually nastier in their behaviour than cats or spiders.

4. Resist feeling guilty about your gardening practices. If you garden with respect for other species (including your neighbours), you have a right to defend yourself against pests. Gardening is a partnership but not a sacrifice. As the French ecologist Gilles Clément puts it: we are all predators, and we are all prey. A garden is a homage to life but death is part of the cycle. Mediterranean cultures are rarely sentimental...

5. Useful versus ornamental: forget this outdated distinction. Instead of ornamental or even productive, think multiple! Not just by including a bit of fashionable potager, but in the variety of the things you grow, the uses you make

of them and the place itself, all day and all year long. Not only for the pleasure of the eyes, but for all the senses.

6. Give free reign to your creative impulses. In the Mediterranean tradition, hands and head are not opposed, nor are manual and mind work, no more than crafts to 'high' art. Designed gardens that are tightly organised around a dominant theme are no better – or worse – than those that depend on serendipity, the gifts of neighbours and of heaven. There are as many styles of garden as there are of poems or paintings.

7. Keep an open mind about what a garden can be. The Mediterranean mixes side by side cosmopolitan show gardens, grandmother's plots and humble allotments. There is no need for envy or scorn for any of these. The important thing is to make one's own choices, not to be a slave of fashion. You can respect the logic and character of the place you live in and still be individually creative, just as you are in cooking.

8. Think local: take advantage of what you have around you. Recycle creatively, but choose materials, textures, colours, volumes that are in harmony with your environment. Avoid visual pollution. Avoid also anonymous features with no local character that can be expensive to maintain, like lawns and certain types of hedging. What plants grow well, in neighbouring gardens or nearby in the wild, which are typical of this place and have prospered here for a long time?

9. Think global: your choices affect the quality of water and of air, and the health of future generations. You are also a caretaker in the 'planetary garden'. As in cooking, make the most of local resources but experiment also with some 'exotics'. Different species become invasive in different environments – check with local experts. Visit other gardens, nearby or far away: you will always learn something useful for home.

10. Think slow: take time to look, sniff, taste and feel. Be open to the unexpected. Be sure there are places to rest in your garden. Lie down on the ground when conditions permit and let a cat lick your fingers. Learn to 'touch and taste peace, silence, unmeasured time, all things which, enjoyed in their excellence, can transform you into a living being you never suspected you really were!' (Jean Giono).

RECOMMENDED READING

Abulafia, David, ed., *The Mediterranean in History*, Thames and Hudson, 2003.

Auden, W.H., 'In Praise of Limestone' in *Collected Shorter Poems, 1922–1957*, Vintage, 1966, pp. 238-40.

Aronson J., Blondel J., Bodiou J.-Y. and Bœuf G. *The Mediterranean Basin – biological diversity in space and time*, Oxford University Press, 2010. See also James Blondel's Restoration Ecology website: www.rncalliance.org

Braudel, Fernand, *The Mediterranean and the Mediterranean World in the Age of Philip II* Vols 1 and 2, Harper Colophon, 1966, first published in 1949.

Cazeille, Adrienne, *Quand on avait tant de racines*, Canet-Roussillon, Editions Trabucaire, 2003.

Clément, Gilles and Louisa Jones, *Gilles Clément: une écologie humaniste*, Aubanel 2006. See also Rocca, Alessandro (below). Plus many other books by Gilles Clément in French: *La Vallée, Manifeste du Tiers-paysage, L'Eloge des vagabondes, Le Salon des berces, La Sagesse du jardinier* etc.

Colette. *Break of Day*, translated by Lisa Allardice, Capuchin Classics, 2011.

Columella, *On Agriculture, Book X: The Layout of the Garden*, translated by E.S. Forster and Edward H. Heffner, Loeb Classical Library Harvard UP, 2001.

Cooper, Guy, and Gordon Taylor, *Mirrors of Paradise: the Gardens of Fernando Caruncho*, Monacelli Press, 2000.

Dallman, Peter R., *Plant Life in the World's Mediterranean Climates*, University of California Press, 1998.

Demoly, Jean-Pierre, and Franklin Picard, *Guide du patrimoine botanique en France*, Actes Sud, 2005.

Durrell, Lawrence, *Spirit of Place: Letters and Essays on Travel*, Ed Alan G. Thomas, Axios Press, 2011.

Eden, Frederick, *A Garden in Venice*, reprint Frances Lincoln, 2003, postface by Marie-Thérèse Weal, first published by Country Life, 1903.

Fabre, Jean-Henri, *The Secret of Everyday Things*, Yesterday's Classics, 2008, excerpts from several books published in French ca. 1900.

Fathy, Hassan, *Natural Energy and Vernacular Architecture: Principles and Examples with Reference to Hot, Arid Climates*, University of Chicago Press, 1986.

Filippi, Olivier, *The Dry Gardening Handbook: Plants and Practices for a Changing Climate*, Thames and Hudson, 2008.

Fortescue, Winifred, *Perfume from Provence*, Black Swan, 1992, first published 1950.

Gay, Jennifer, *Greece: Garden of the Gods,* Athens News, 2004.

Gildemeister, Heidi, *Gardening the Mediterranean Way: Practical Solutions forSummer-dry Climates,* Thames and Hudson, 2004.

Gildemeister, Heidi, *Mediterranean Gardening: A Waterwise Approach,* Editorial Moll, 1998.

Giono, Jean, *The Man Who Planted Trees,* Chelsea Green Publishing, 2007, first published 1953. Plus many novels and essays.

Goldsworthy, Andy, *Time,* Abrams, 2008.

Graves, William, *Wild Olives: Life in Majorca with Robert Graves,* Pimlico, 2001.

Grove, A.T. and Rackham, Oliver, *The Nature of Mediterranean Europe: An Ecological History,* Yale University Press, 2003.

Hallé, François, *In Praise of Plants,* Timber Press, 2011, first published 1999.

Harbouri, Caroline Ed., *The Mediterranean Garden,* journal of the Mediterranean Garden Society.

Harbouri, Petrie, *Our Lady of the Serpents,* Bloomsbury Publishing, 1999.

Harris, W.V. ed. *Rethinking the Mediterranean,* Oxford University Press 2005.

Hesiod, *The Homeric Hymns,* and *Homerica,* ed. & translator Hugh G. Evelyn-White, Loeb Classics, Harvard University Press, 1914.

Highet, Gilbert, *Poets in a Landscape,* New York Review of Books Classics, 2010, first published 1957.

Homer, *The Odyssey,* trans. Samuel Butler, Barnes and Noble, 1993.

Horden, Peregrine and Purcell, Nicholas, *The Corrupting Sea: a Study of Mediterranean History,* Blackwell Publishing, 2000.

Hunt, John Dixon. *The Venetian City Garden: Place typology and perception,* Birkhauser Boston, 2009.

Huxley, Aldous, *The Olive Tree and other essays,* Chatto and Windus, 1947.

Jones, Louisa, for books in English, see page x.

Leach, Helen, *Cultivating Myths: Fiction, Fact and Fashion in Garden History,* Godwit, 2000.

Lieutaghi, Pierre, *Trees: The Balance of Life, The Beauty of Nature,* Duncan Baird 2011. Plus many books in French : *Badasson & Cie : Tradition médicinale et autres usages des plantes en haute Provence*; *Petite Ethnobotanique méditerranéenne, Jardins du chêne blanc.*

Mabey, Richard, *Weeds: In Defence of Nature's Most Unloved Plants,* Ecco, 2011.

Martineau, Alice, *Gardening in Sunny Lands,* D. Appleton and Company, 1924.

Maurières, Arnaud and Ossart, Eric, *Paradise Gardens,* Editions du Chêne, 2001.

Mure, Véronique, *Jardins de Garrigue,* Edisud, 2007.

Nottle, Trevor, *Gardens of the Sun,* Timber Press, 1996.

Page, Russell, *The Education of a Gardener,* The Harville Press, London, 1994, first published 1962.

Pagnol, Marcel, *Jean de Florette & Manon of the Springs,* North Point Press, 1988, first published 1963.

Papanek, Victor, *The Green Imperative: Ecology and Ethics in Design and Architecture,* Thames and Hudson, 1995.

Pearson, Dan, *Garden Inspiration,* Fuel, 2009.

Pérez-Vitoria, Silvia, *Les Paysans sont de retour,* Actes Sud, 2005 and *La riposte des paysans,* Actes Sud, 2010.

Pliny the Younger, *Letters,* trans. William Melmoth, revised by F.C.T. Bosanquet, Harvard Classics, P.F. Collier & Son, 1909.

Pitte, Jean-Robert, *French Gastronomy,* Columbia University Press, 2002.

Ponge, Francis, *The Nature of Things,* Red Dust Inc, 1995 and *Comment une figue de paroles et pourquoi,* Garnier Flammarion, 1999, originally published1955.

Rabhi, Pierre and Yehudi Menuhin, *As in the Heart, So in the Earth: Reversing the Desertification of the Soul and the Soil,* Park Street Press, 2006. See also in French *Vers la sobriété heureuse,* Actes Sud 2010 and many more.

Rocca, Alessandro, *Planetary Gardens: the Landcape Architecture of Gilles Clément* Birkhäuser Architecture, 2008.

Serre, Olivier de, *Théâtre d'agriculture et mesnage des champs,* Actes Sud 1997, originally published 1600.

Sitwell, Sir George. *The Making of Gardens,* Daniel R. Godine, 2003, first published 1909.

Tyrwhitt, Mary Jaqueline, *Making a Garden on a Greek Hillside.* Denise Harvey, http://www.deniseharveypublisher.gr/, 2012, first published 1998.

Van Gogh, Vincent, *The Complete Letters: With Reproductions of All the Drawings in the Correspondence,* ed. Leo Jansen, Hans Luijten et Nienke Bakker, Actes Sud, 2009. See also http://www.vangoghletters.org/vg/

Virgil, *Georgics* Book 1, translation H. R. Fairclough. See http://www.theoi.com/Text/VirgilGeorgics1.html#1.

Von Arnim, Elizabeth, *The Enchanted April,* New York Review Books Classics, 2007, first published in 1922.

Wharton, Edith, *Italian Villas and their Gardens,* Ulan Press, 2012, first published 1903.

ACKNOWLEDGMENTS

The scientific underpinning of this book comes from one major source: the recently published, definitive book on Mediterranean biodiversity (see recommended books under Blondel). One of its authors, James Aronson, was particularly generous in sharing his work with me even before publication. Dan Pearson took time from preparing a major exhibit on his work at the Garden History museum to write the preface, much appreciated. Pierre Lieutaghi, practically the founder of French ethnobotany, wrote a poetic and most generous preface for the French edition. Warwick Forge has been dauntless in his faith in this book, leading to its publication in English, thanks also to the generous and excellent professional copy-editing of Caroline Harbouri. This book sums up well over thirty years of garden experience and reflection. A complete list of all those who have helped and inspired me in that time would be impossible to establish though I am grateful to all. But among them, I most wish to thank Jean-Marie Rey, Roseline Bacou, Yves Coutarel, William Waterfield, Yves Delange, Bruno Goris, Nicole Martin-Raget and Doudou Bayol. Many professional designers – especially Dominique Lafourcade, Jean Mus, Michel Semini and Alain David Idoux, and now the following generation – have given unstintingly of their precious time in order to show me their recent work. Nicole de Vésian and Marc Nucera became almost family. In recent years, my thinking has been nourished constantly by exchanges with Gilles Clément, Olivier Filippi, Heidi Gildemeister, Arnaud Maurières and Eric Ossart as well as with members of certain associations such as the Ecologistes de l'Euzière and the Mediterranean Garden Society. The list of colleagues, writers and photographers to whom I owe a great deal would take many pages, but I note especially Vincent Motte, my first photographer, whose early demise we all much regret. I have also known many publishers, most (but not all) committed and scrupulous. The most intelligently helpful editor over a long period has certainly been Jamie Camplin of Thames and Hudson. In my earliest days, Annie François at the Editions du Seuil, though she never in fact published me, gave generously of her time and advice, especially with my French. In my books with Actes Sud, I have had the immense privilege of working with Aïté Bresson and thank her once again for her efficiency, intelligence, patience and kindness.

PHOTO CREDITS

Front cover by Clive Nichols (www.clivenichols.com).
Page 18 and 54 by Vincent Motte (mireillemotte@live.fr).
Pages 42, 62, 110, 120, 134 by Beatrice Pichon-Clarisse (bpichon.clarisse@gmail.com).
Back cover by Monique Mailloux (monique@yriaparos.com).
Front flap portrait of author by Sophie Baker.
All other photos are by Louisa Jones.

Original French edition © 2012, Actes Sud France
Le Méjan, Place Nina Berberova
13200 Arles, France
www.actes-sud.fr

English hardback edition published 2013 by
Bloomings Books Pty Ltd
Melbourne, Australia
T (03) 9804 8915
E warwick@bloomings.com.au
www.landscapeconference.com

Bloomings Books is a specialist publisher
of gardening and natural history books.

Text © Louisa Jones 2013
English translation © Louisa Jones 2013
Images © 2013

All rights reserved. No part of this publication may be reproduced, stored in or introduced into a
retrieval system, or transmitted in any form or by any means (electronic, mechanical, photocopying,
recording or otherwise), without the prior written permission of the copyright owner and publishers.
Enquiries should be addressed to the publishers.

National Library of Australia Cataloguing-in-Publication data:

Jones, Louisa E., author.

Mediterranean gardens : a model for good living / Louisa Jones.

9780992290092 (hardback)

Includes bibliographical references.

Gardening.
Gardens--Design.
Gardens--Styles.

712

Cover design and typesetting: Pfisterer+Freeman
Printer: Printed in China by Everbest Printing Co Ltd